vetiver

poems by

librecht baker

Finishing Line Press
Georgetown, Kentucky

vetiver

Copyright © 2017 by librecht baker
ISBN 978-1-63534-322-9 First Edition
All rights reserved under International and Pan-American Copyright Conventions. No part of this book may be reproduced in any manner whatsoever without written permission from the publisher, except in the case of brief quotations embodied in critical articles and reviews.

ACKNOWLEDGMENTS

Emerge: 2015 Lambda Literary Fellows Anthology includes "you echo the blessing of rebellion (for Black Lives Matter)" and "us kind." "phantom gun: murdered by police and counting" can be read on the *THANK YOU FOR SWALLOWING* website (issue 2.2, 2016). *Writing the Walls Down: A Convergence of LGBTQ Voices* (Trans-Genre Press, 2015) anthologized "to descend upon ourselves." Lastly, "stories great-aunt Ethel keeps" is included in *Bone Bouquet* issue (8.1, 2017).

"carry we forward" includes the text from a 2016 Facebook post by Natasha Marin. "you echo the blessing of rebellion (for Black Lives Matter)" includes text from Suheir Hammad's poem and short film "Into Egypt" (2011). "mother primordial" includes text from Ashaki M. Jackson's poem "The Anterior *(or* The Pidgin She Taught Us)" from *Language Lesson* (Miel, 2016).

Publisher: Leah Maines

Editor: Christen Kincaid

Cover Art: "She Who Dwells at the Cove" by artist Sydney "Sage Stargate" Cain

Author Photo: Vivian Allen/VONA

Cover Design: Elizabeth Maines McCleavy

Printed in the USA on acid-free paper.
Order online: www.finishinglinepress.com
also available on amazon.com

Author inquiries and mail orders:
Finishing Line Press
P. O. Box 1626
Georgetown, Kentucky 40324
U. S. A.

roots of content

Acknowledgments

cry/call
ancestor (one) 1
being as we is.. 2
other (than strong black womyn) blackness............................. 3
carry me forward... 5

scream/response
monsters aren't under the bed: whiteness and sex 9
vetiver 13
why didn't the militia in oregon, occupying malheur national
    wildlife refuge, put cork paint on their face before squatting
    on land they can never own—land of the Burns Paiute people ... 15
phantom gun: murdered by police and counting...................... 17

faint/release
imitation 21
falling bodies (one) 23
for us... 25
river, rot, rise 27
dear (273) 28
conversation with myself.. 29
mother primordial.. 33
war horse 34
bedlam creation 35
Baker 36
when act I, homage is televised and act II, critique is erased
    in 1981.. 38
elder tears 40

collected/rising
begin blessing... 43
deep pussy 44
haiti, bless you.. 46
pools (47)... 47
grow/weed along/vine over clenching my own truth 48
where's Betty Mabry Davis 50

Sinaa 51
dear Sinaa 53
stories great-aunt Ethel keeps 54
indigo ~~haiku~~ 57
penumbra tableau 58

waking up together
to descend upon ourselves 63
you echo the blessing of rebellion (for Black Lives Matter) 65
us kind 66
falling bodies (two) 69
may the dead in you rise 73

Thank You 75

cry/call

ancestor (one)

i suppose memories of we make them ashamed,
but they forget which of us they grabbed, traded, gifted to wind & sea

sure my titties hang low, but some of my children
their titties hang lower and they never worked like i

i work/worked, are my children beckoned upon as i
i was conditioned to always be ready, but some of our children move slow

slower than their memories being erased, they repeat always
what is erased, they move with their blood of our blood

some of my children are tired of hearing/listening/reading
about our bound passage through ocean's middle bringing we to americas

some of our children have forgotten we know navigation
we had/have many ocean rites of passage prior to and after

for what reason do our children have to be ashamed
we are many herstories beyond that moment

yet they are conditioning themselves to erase us because
they are tired of hearing/listening/reading about *it*

we were born abundantly wealthy moreso than *it*
and during *it* some of we were abundant, subversive, resilient

aware or not, we echo in their chest
and we are not ashamed of steps we left and led

they, our children, are echoes of our echoes calling response
all of we in their chest are calling them

continue to hear/listen/read/speak about we
we are more than you know/own/believe

continue to make more of we so you shall be seen seeing yourself

being as we is

pushing back against imaginary walls manifested dangerously
or
pushing back against imaginary walls manifested dangerously
feeding the kash grass within because blooming may autumn once
                      there will always be monsoons upon us
trill twilight's bright gleam with earth's turn to sunrise

other (than strong black womyn) blackness

Black is the Color of My True Love's Hair blackness spell me
Alice's *Fool for You* echoing blackness sing me
They Say I'm Different owning blackness me
THEESatisfaction astro black space dark matter me
Mickalene Thomas drafting rhinestone, acrylic, enamel blackness tint me
Zanele Muholi make memory blackness snap me
Alicia Garza, Opal Tometi, Patrisse Cullors pushback, wade and chant blackness me
trinity blackness as eyes-shut cosmic-ether reflection
womyn without words unwilling me permission to crumble
meteor shower sheening black bursting detritus
through blackness, like an etheric binding
tears release where shrilling scream may come
blackness undone, permit me
i permission pleasure in calling forth names
other than commonly called strong black womyn, such as
trembling tenderly
durable duplicitous alienation
sorbet complexity strolling slowly in this history
vetiver violet variation
yes yielding a yard of yams yearnings for only yes
names as
willing water lily wielding wild stems and mud
nesting nourishment needed, always
opulent orgasmer and organizer
delphinium dipped
allspice however sleek and sour
many moods amidst midnight myrrh
copal contoured with cacophony
more names like
hole in the ship impingement and mobility
bleeding bergamot—depression antidepressant
daily duality walking with dualities
blessed bleeding yes mess blessed
standing zephyr song
shield me save worthy
glorification of and then sell blackness to myself(s)

devil's claw claiming self-care
blackjoyousass betty
thrilling them titillatingly
poinsettia points of departure
flowerage and flowing fluid identity while exuding flagrance
or other names as
pretty peasant being
anticipated antics against
intuitive keen kisser
self-suture exhibitionist
rushing river of reverence
knowledgeable kindred of kite sky gliding
butchness marks her miles
master/mistress of variant vernacular (code) switch
dismantler of romanticized picket fences
permission pleasure in calling forth names
other than the three words we are
constrained and
consistently called
blackness spell me
while being erotically other(ed)
as a supreme being at will
to be supreme requires willingness

carry we forward
     after Natasha Marin

what crisis do i have that's carrying me forward, i
hold me inside its calamities that aren't supposed to exist, but do incessantly come
as a sweet jasmine gust with yesterday's yesterday stories dragging from
old wounds unremembered, legacies becoming a
wider weary worry, worries where wounds are unattended to as people
carrying memories forward as memories forget they are forgotten, however, known
and passed forth habitually through blood-memory for
life isn't happenstances breeding,
but awoken old oaths, cyclical meanderings and innovation
reaching from
unattended spirits, when we don't do our personal work, we pass forth crisis

scream/response

monsters aren't under the bed: whiteness and sex

in america there are two monsters: whiteness and sex
at times they become one entity leading to a hyperbolic point: example, cisgender white monster(s) engages nonconsensual sex with a person(s), another white monster(s) grants them access with no jail time to roam and eat more people

example, 1704 south carolina created patty rollers aka "enslavers of all non-cisgender white beings because patty rollers are ultimate impunity," patty rollers hire(d) and clone(d) their origins: picnic lynch mobs, police sectors, attorney generals, prisons, lawyers, monsantos etc., but bear witness to your mind, some monsters hunt their own and create colored monsters

example, identity(s) can only be survived by fellating social constructs
thus, the birth of murdering queer people and unacknowledged homophobic hate crimes, black bodies seen as holy beasts to be capsized, continuous genocide of native american people, and raping prostitutes seen as an expected action because they earn money in an alternate economy

americans aren't to own ourselves with consensual, occasional, at-will freedom fucks between beings enjoying licking one another's taste

the monsters aren't under our bed, they've conditioned us to condition ourselves and exist in autopilot mode where certain stripes stand while other stripes hang off a ledge and all the stars get lambasted for representing the real america it will always be: a complex culture and complexions showing culture at first sight. america's flat ass is often shown eating itself

between stripes and stars is threading woven so that we can't breathe, when we attempt to making a living by living, when we knock on a neighbor's door for help, when we are given a dose of bullets to the body in the backseat of a paddywagon while handcuffed, or when we walk in our neighborhood being sexualized by porch-perched cats reacting angrily when rejected

example, white hood impunity is same excuse upholding blue lives murdering and receiving paid desk assignments post-murder, despite dash and body cameras and citizens' valiant observation. should blue lives' attire be hung in the national museum of african american history and culture because their histories reflect disengagement with people of color?

orgasms creep upward, watering flesh body in bursting, tingling illumination, a twilight-worn desire, despite *big black dicks* being a primary internet search, *this* big black bigness remains as a funeral casket post-whiteness' ejaculated limp and ogling sufficed, big and black becomes an *it* and desirable feelings buried, forgotten until next night, does whiteness hunger in dawn's light?

example, picture of Sandra Bland in waller county, texas orange jumpsuit shrouding shoulders and chest against concrete backdrop, her sugar-glazed eyes un-alert and face slacken reflects photographer's camera's gaze—when are mugshots *not* taken in street clothes—mugshots show a person's revolting spirit, unless their stare is one of their spirit escaping a dying body

specimen ad nauseam, 2016 elections highlight our country's throbbing essence—divisiveness celebrated in the election of a trashbag president-elect, son of a white hood, how *pledge allegiance to the flag*, how sweet *bombs bursting in air,* how unripe lemon tangy, so spit into the hot multicultural pot holding our country's chunky organic-monsanto stew

and what does the popular vote mean anyway, why is it called a popular vote, if its popularity isn't winning

sample, 40.2 percent of our poverty population is white-america, what is talk box saying, what is national newspaper informing about our poverty? only discussing poverty stricken people looking like deportation, a jail case, migratory, worth bordering, pepper spraying, to be slain, and what about the 40.2 percent—grief and hunger, an experienced shared in breath carried by wind

fear mongers greet 2016 election triumphant-deficit with a self-sworn badge to harass *the others* while waving ghost era flag that zombie forth eating statue of liberty's full, fleshy nose to a sliver—they've forgotten they're a handful of generations removed from immigrant status and their history is championed by the public educational system, but only some monsters read

is it to be afraid of *the others* and so needing *the others*—hungry for cultures, exoticism, seasoned foods with the tastes of certain histories—simultaneously the legacy of monsters and what happens when monsters doesn't comprehend their own monstrosity

here, there's no question mark because onslaught has no end—this is part true of our america

illustrated best where whiteness distracts us from ourselves or whiteness is too distracted from itself—its love, its history, its compassion—it/they/she/he have spent a long time trying to not remember and aide our memories' oblivion, but what would we expect from a *color* that is the end result of all colors spinning—has their spinning encouraged forgetting that roots grow in dark

selling brutality stories about us clashing with, assaulting, and murdering police, but what is more common is obvious—where police are present at peaceful rebellions so too is centuries of energy glimmering, off their dehydrated, piss color badge and riot gear—police bringing assault, murder, and clash against citizens, but what about the hungry 40.2 percent

and what about water, air, earth

america has always been great, no election or next president-elect can shift obvious fact that we are a country of immigrants—except the indigenous who know america's birth name(s)—however, generationally removed, the majority of us eat with a tongue split by its psychological diet where english has always been the forced first spoonful

monsters thrive by diverting incendiary focus. they are antebellum wannabes and as ugly as ever with a terror litany palette—america knows its terrorist candor and acts like the terrorists are the darkies over there, points finger, points finger and points finger across the sea, in the ghetto, shanty towns, places where survival seems to be thin and always fighting

in america, we know there is no salvation for non-monsters unless *the others* create it without fear of becoming, while enjoying consensual fucking-loving making-celibacy in due process of self-designated law and order and for all america's greatness, what has made america great is there will never be a thriving single story because a hyphen always precedes america

a dissimilar-symbiotic relationship

vetiver

i never cry like i want to
heaving over pain welled up for years
reasons fluid-filled sacs visit beneath flesh where
pain squanders sadness of *i got to find away out of here* heaviness
because bodies keep falling
we watch the fallings recorded by bystanders and dash and body cameras
bodies keep falling
no cream, bandaid or pill able to make immunity to the fallings
falling as we fall
shot down while asking for help
in head, burst open like rotted, soft, mushy yams
as hands in surrender falling last, after breath falls first
where voices call and none respond to
again, head kicked in like an old hallow eve's pumpkin
handcuffed, subdued or hogtied and quiet
falling, made to fall
where is the instant relief

and neediness to scream gravelly, hard until
the *falling stops*
and i pass out from exhaustion, from vomit coming upward because videos keep coming
       and what about our bodies falling that we never hear about
       left
              s
            w
          a
         y
          i
            n
              g
or lockdown down in solitary confinement and thrown food, even though they can't move so
body dies as spirit lingers feeling
    i'm
        not
            dead

am i not dead, who gone
r   e   l   e   a   s   e   me
who   gone   r   e   l   e   a   s   e
            me
so i can scream
and it's not only men (cis-gender)
it's all of us identities—trans   cis   fluid   hetero   queer   in-question   bi spectrum etc.
elsewhere there is us who is poor   disabled   mentally blended   veterans with ptsd   parents   children   somebody's person   a person
but all of us aren't rallied for like them floating in the binary
if we do, mainstream pisses its stream with its 'i am shit and i eat shit because i like shit' grin

i wish i could vomit
at least it would satisfy the scream i can't seem to do alone—by myself
when
am i gonna
r   e   l   e   a   s   e
there's no translation for grief i carry
same grief we all carry
beyond borders of flesh, labels, and lack, we all begin and continue energetically in one place: darkness
because inside
your momma is black

why didn't the militia in oregon, occupying malheur national wildlife refuge, put cork paint on their face before squatting on land they can never own—land of the Burns Paiute people

it'd be so jazz—grinning makes receptivity easier
so entertaining—paris expatriate
so terrorist extremist—fanatics said to be darker hues, but what about that blue
so thrilling still life—paint the bodies on the floor
so national guard for safety
so disco—cocaine
so 1980s—reagan shipping in foreign crack, then implementing a crack era
so sensationalist—can't eat gmo breakfast, while reading newspaper
so ghetto tenements—buildings not people
so cotton picking prisoners—work for cents and no pension
so texas—let's pump oil
so american media—fear tactics and pro-israel
so propaganda—believe everything without question
so terrorist extremist, again—home soil trained and funded
so protester like—there are no marchers here, only people named anti-american
so bleach white gloves, watermelon fleshy lips, and bulging low iq eyes
so civil rights, voter registration, and lack of free healthcare—have two inmates
    beat Fannie
so welfare, electronic benefit transfer, general relief—40.2 percent welfare
    queens are white
so vietnam and laos—20 years greed
so christmas day in somalia
so lapband surgery
so remote controlled—controlled self-control
so standing rock—police arresting prayers and sirening their beloved sound
    cannon hymns
that's so look at me—insta-everything
so belo monte dam in brazil—kill all who remember nature
so papua new guinea—torturing, gasoline and setting aflame Kepari, a womyn
    labeled
so orgasmic—the gun is making us tremble all over
so peruvian—burn Rosa alive and burn her body for three days
it's so look at me—i feel insecure, i need likes
so boogie woogie—let's twist like us and them standards
so tulsa, oklahoma 1921—burn a bourgeoning community

so monsanto parasitic, chemical creatures—birth once seeds, while birthing
    infections
that's so famous—how much did it cost you to be seen
so mississippi goddamn
so rape culture
so unemployment benefits—two years became six months limit
so anti-human right's campaign—how many transgender folks have been
    murdered
so divisive—don't write about the natives, asians, latinxs, whites, pacific
    islanders killed by blue
so wet pussy—grab them no questions asked
so wounded knee—what treaty was signed and fucked by colonial america on
    repeat
so red cross—millions collect with haiti's name bannering, but haiti didn't
    receive
so what—throw it up, throw it up, this base low
so new orleans—fema didn't offer healing, after the levees broke
so coca cola—manufactured sugar induced happiness
so abortion clinic—womyn need escorts for their health's safety
so white man—hunt anything different
so big corporation—wells fargo, citibank, ing bank, icbc london, bank of
    america, crédit agricole
    and the other bitches funding native & nature's destruction
so ass fat—let's crank for celebrated superficiality and disconnect

phantom gun: murdered by police and counting

open palms trigger no spit shiny gun
judicial system disallows truth say
badge shimmers, aims, shoots hue, skin conundrum

streets become open caskets, we can't run
blockade, gather, protest onward display
open palms trigger no spit shiny gun

lit candles, wilting bouquets cascade hum
concrete catches blooming fruit, open grave
badge shimmers, aims, shoots hue, skin conundrum

bodies pass forth memories harsh like sun
rebel winter turn spring, standing flags fray
open palms trigger no spit shiny gun

raze all replicas, american drum
murky stories, phantom gun they carry
badge shimmers, aims, shoots hue, skin conundrum

witness given no refuge, must run
for life, recollecting they do marry
open palms trigger no spit shiny gun
badge shimmers, aims, shoots hue, skin conundrum

faint/release

imitation

2016 flood in louisiana begin in one place: ~~weather modification~~
                        classism
                        lack of access
                        sexism
                        xenophobia
                        homophobia
                        heteronormativity
                        actualized structural racism
                        truth of the matter of isms
                        impulse of supremacy

                                              a place/dimension seen and unseen
                                            there are footnotes as proof and
                                            summation(s) of capitalistic creations

flood began in one place and this place

                                            inaccessible grounds

creates erasure and succeeds, except for the
body—lineage—experience culture memory
and its elevation

                                            inaccessible grounds cannot contend
                                            with cultural memory

however, flood imitates many forces:
                        2004 bp oil spill (earth-wound-purge)
                        2005 katrina & new orleans' levees breaking
                        2016 petroperú's amazon rainforest crude oil spill
                        2016 rds oil spill, again near louisiana
                        (earth ruptures from greed)

flood in louisiana began in one place

dakota access pipeline idea began in one place:

        an impulse of supremacy
        intention to destroy and suppress communities
        frame circumstances creating more monetary blood
        income (earth wound continuously bursting)

dakota access pipeline and floods began in one place: in mouths
        discussing an irreversible deluge against people
        blathering disregard for indigenous sovereign land
        refuting people who know america's pre-colonial names
        levitated by suit & ties on inaccessible grounds
        of ceos of 17 banks using our money to oppress others
                to stock their plantations

here, oil and water mix

        drowning biodiversity
        sewaging water supply
        plundering sacrosanct land
        wounding knees of next generations

may the remaining 40 percent of the pipeline never be built to completion

falling bodies (one)

these black, brown bodies falling
falling black, brown bodies
we are not always falling, counted
seen as many falling, that all we do
is fall
    fall
      and fall
        falling to fail
           failing so we fall
in life
in love
in place
      falling is our place
our place is to be out of place
what is there to adjust if
          our place is seen binded
                    internally
out of place(s)
we are perceived as womb-less
full of wounds
        power in the words we breathe
          power to healing a place
touch we tender
we have a place
        place is not misaligned
what is energy of the center
center is governing system with
          its domineering racial lens
            center of conditioned conditioning
some of us believe in center
so we seem infused with failing, falling, and no place
are we hurt
    born to hurt
        born to hurt others
no
we are born
    born to birth a place

      born into a place
born intentionally
      intentionally of passionate pulse
a place birthing

for us

1.
the black male is not
only american prey
there's no single story

black men are not the
only americans to pray for
there's no single story

cis-gender black men
aren't the beginning-end of
our american story

2.
becoming anointed
and slayed in america's name
scat singing stories

hollowing prece-
dent repeats quilted patterns'
patchwork stitched stories

recurrent beliefs
of self-willed conditioning
ecotone stories

3.
if we are anointed
slayed in the name of, tell our
self-birthed name stories

our american
beginning-end isn't sickly
white picket fences

divergent normal
cross spectrum identity

american stories

4.
america's prey
is a glance in the reflect-
ing pool, pray we dip

every birth has a
hyphen, poverty, crime, skin
is pipeline stories

for all ourselves lost
because americans murdered
them, repeat their names

5.
people people pe-
ople continue repeat pe-
ople, people people

river, rot, rise

a barren river is a river—temperamental
tithing herself an unwoven basket
struck by her flow—forgetting her river(s)
fall from sky and sky pours from her
primordial black, reaching moon blood
roots, turning over where rot
so rot can rise from her rot, birthing
reaping, consecrating self in her continuance
no one may benefit if she dis-members her flow
or is restrained by other's broken fallen branches
obligating her currents so she forgets
her mandatory discharge, necessary effusion
binding creek, overriding currents reaching
running, rescuing, recalling, reclaiming, re-collects
her river is a river of an ocean's memories calling
her, so she is divined to respond and midwife
becoming a new lineage, a new delta

dear (273)

dear ibeji aunties,

in the moments when your brother not once, but twice asked you make a patriarchal-misogyny-encased in homophobia phone call requesting that my spouse and i not attend family functions, did you consider telling him to make his own phone call?

or the 13th baby of Lillie Mae and Glover Williams should not act child-baby like?

or that your phone call would return me unwanted to trauma's door?

or encourage depression?

or trigger an emotional asthma attack—a sense of breathing through an orange-red cocktail straw?

or create a feeling of being unprotected, again, from a man in our family?

or? or? or?

did you consider that you are not the second and third person your brother asked to make a patriarchal-misogyny-encased in homophobia phone call?

the first person he asked was tennessee cousin, your nephew, to call and talk to me about changing my mind about being who i am. i'm unsure what that request means. although tennessee didn't side with your brother, hearing your brother's request from tennessee was like two storm cells clashing in new mexico's sky—omnipresent, ashen, dusty. have you ever seen that or felt it inside of you?

do you know ifa's meaning of the birth of ibeji?

conversation with myself

family people are supposed to remember your significant other is significant to you and should be counted in the number of limited people invited to the birthday gathering, right?

yes.

was october twenty-second, two thousand sixteen the last you time you attend a family gathering, without the person you've chosen to build a family with?

yes.

why is your answer yes?

because when they forget and i arrive alone, i feel heart-pain when i witness clumps of family people and their significant other present—i don't feel alone, only excluded and—

why do you feel excluded?

my commitment to my spouse is unwelcomed, intentionally or unintentionally. yes because my other half cries sadness all over the house. becomes deflated. their blackjoyousness disappears.

how do you express commitment when you too are excluding your significant other by attending the celebration…alone? weren't your actions reflective of the family member who intentionally or unintentionally didn't plus one you?

yes. i wasn't honoring my chosen binding nor being complete with myself. i wasn't on october twenty-second, two thousand sixteen

what happened when you arrived at the party?

family people said *i thought you weren't coming, where's your significant other. i've heard so much about her. i'd like to meet her*, and *where's your friend.*

how did that make you feel?

deflated.

what does that mean?

what does what mean?

you said you felt deflated. what does that mean?

i knew grief would be waiting for me at home.

whose grief?

hers. mine. ours. together it's suffocating. grief and disagreement.

what was the disagreement about?

attending the party alone. she did say i should be present because my brother and his pregnant fiancé would be there, even though—

wasn't she speaking a coded language?

yes.

and you speak in codes, but you missed the patterns in her tongue. right?

yes.

what happened after you misread the code?

suffocated.

what will you do to prevent suffocating?

never october twenty-second, two thousand sixteen at six forty-five post meridian, again.

why?

we are too valuable to self-inflict pain. i drink blackjoyousness regularly. agony can be its own company

why?

she's my only.

why?

i made a vow.

what was your vow and for whom?

myself. myself care. walk my path, even when the earth trembles me.

yes. she trembles to release. what does that mean to you?

i have to release…

what do you have to release?

this is not what i expected.

what did you expect? you and i both knew the first outcome, after you began trembling.

i knew. yes, i knew, but i didn't expect any family person to react, but…i knew.

what will you do with your knowing, now?

try to forget. not suffocate. remember blackjoyouness and my only. not wait for any family person to accept the aspect of myself that i will always wear. you know, i have a garden?

yes, but some plants are suffocating.

i know.

are you ready to repot your mint, succulent, and lemon tree?

yes.

it's time. don't you agree?

yes.

mother primordial
    after Ashaki M. Jackson

hard guttural bliss-less wailing stuck inside my pussy, latched to root
waiting for release, how can release know to release me/we for
mother's moist earth, wet tongue invoking me/we, mother

if i lose my unearthed reach/grasp/clench/belly's umbilical hold to you, how can my root
lead/lean in direction without a trunk-worth of knowing for-
ward my breath becomes stagnant, when inside me i lose you, mother

my memory, how do i beckon remember to re-member trunk-root, when we
forget/oblivious spirit's innate birthright root
our reach/clench/grasp/belly's umbilical hold for
one another, we reflect in walking flesh our wish for mother

's primordial core darken, from lack of sun/moonlight, waters root
every we begin again encased in dark matters inside skin, for
the intuit, lullabies, and belonging begins there, how can i/we return to mother

when we/i disremember our root-
truth-journey for ourselves from ourselves calling for-
th knowing that resembles a diversion from self, an undesirable ghost, mother

of your many names, which do i/we call you to call upon you and root
within, re-umbilical beyond the eclipse i/we birth, when we for-
get, though continuously move with fear of self, mother

how can i/we bond continuously with our origins when i/we forget our root

war horse

the spirit of war is not your spirit
war is a thrust: conditioned and pushed into you

bedlam creation

and what about bedlam creation pushing us to center
displacement from ourselves to regenerate
our displaced self, a ligament joining yearning and becoming self

how much can chaos hold if its disorder is unstable
feeble in its spinning and unable to be one
with its displaced self, what is chaos reaching for

our vulnerability because we don't want our distance seen
between our stagnancy and destined point—our catalyst
private place when we are untamed, spinning, lightening

and becoming, however, on our journey(s)

when we are surviving, spilling, losing our mask(s)
is when we should be seen, in our moments
collaging and painting our self into being and

celestially invoking

Baker

last name distance
like a car ride from long beach, california to columbus, georgia
with no freezer breezing air conditioner, busted window crank roll up handle
and brows sweat as hands piously wipe away clear glass beads with a handkerchief
31 hours or 2,172.80 miles via i-10 east through arizona's skeletal heart
from port city to unknown
perhaps, great-grandmother Sarah is still living

from long beach, califorinia to opelika, alabama
riding greyhound bus sitting near toilet's jasmine stench
while neighbor passenger dreams home
nestling upon plush couch, my shoulder
Williams last name gifts more, but queen of the heavens has no reign
so Baker takes ownership like a dog shitting in its feeding bowl, whining of hunger
31 hours or 2,158.80 miles via i-10 east through bottoms of arizona
grandma Gladys is buried here, in long beach, after cancer ate her

vastness, vacuous last name
grandfather Johnny, in his eldership went to jail for domestic violence against his second wife, an oily orange-brown faint Gladys replica
uncle Kennard is *somewhere*
dad, Mel, lives on cedar avenue philosophizing with his art five minutes from me—we commune banshee
uncle Johnny—i haven't crossed his crossed welcoming bridge

our name means we don't recognize when we are trifling
becoming infinitesimal because we don't colony communing as californian argentine ants
trailing their colony from the outside crevices into our bathroom
from under sink looking for water and trashed food
argentines discover, kiss in passing, pass information to one another returning to home colony
i have chosen not to kiss my colony

but in *Immigration Essays* you planted a gift
packaged by your unpacking of

The History of the Baker Family, your family name
my family brass—too heavy with time (re)name(d)
a name i carry grudgingly
you wrote the Bakers came from england to georgia in 1700s
my great-grandmother Sarah, skin twilight smile colored, live(d) in georgia
although american education swirls its alcoholic claim
not all black americans scion from enslaved africans
many *They Came Before Columbus*
others are 711 anno domini reincarnates with leukotomy memory
i wonder if the *two negro nurses* working *in a Confederate hospital*
your great-great grandfather wrote of in 1863
gave me this blood i let each month
did your great-great-grandfather's folk corral my people
or is the Baker name as common as americans smiling while grieving *

---

* "The History of the Baker Family" in *Immigration Essays* by Sybil Baker (C&R Press, 2017)

when act I, homage is televised and act II, critique is erased in 1981
in acknowledgement of Ben Vereen

i saw you once at Nita's house, Ben
your smiling hello, a sentient ravine both welcoming water & sustaining evergreen without it
carrying you, a revival of shooting stars skittering a human canopy

if you're someone welcomed into the home of Nita, a person whose heart & voice reaches skyward like redwoods, then you're someone whose spirit glimmers

when i saw you, i was unaware of
    1981's inauguration performance
    act I and act II
    homage and critique
    Bert Williams and you

but i knew about blackface and minstrelling and blackface's minstrel history

Babylon Girls: Black Women Performers Shaping of the Modern made me bidialectal

and i know how we
    have to embody our bodies to perform our bodies' magic, history, lineages,
        and adoration
            and the scars
                the scars, sometimes
                    we're the only person adept to carriaging communal scars

had Arceneaux not created *Until, Until, Until...*, i still would be unaware of
    Bert Williams and you
    homage and critique
    act I and act II
    1981 and appearance(s)

yet, i will never be aware of your scars
    their size and taste
        however, possibly healed

sometimes

it takes us generations to understand how we perform
    how we carry each other's worth, while valuing ourselves
        how we witness and respond to those of you who carry
            honor us
                and critiques the past
                      while uplifting one of our own

dear elder tears

you've decide to be afraid because we've begun
unblinking our eyes, seeing you and us equal

we see you in us, us as you
and you no longer perched unreachable upon a plinth

we see you
how do you see us?

we speak language(s) we learned from you
why do you cover our tongues with earth?

we know us as you
why do platter us with molasses, cayenne, and salty distance?

we link arms cheering you,
but you shamed and separated us, when we disagree with you

running farthest as an outcast crone,
but you are the caster of your own belly stones

what you fear is not us, dearest elder
do you fear your candle's flame dimming or disempowerment?

or us unveiling ourselves to ourselves, resting in our own lap and not yours?
and fortuitously we'll offer ourselves our own blessing

you taught us to trust what we hear,
but you've decided we should only trust hearing you

you taught us to honor our teachers' teaching and make
our own path, so what about us plagues you?

dearest elder, you can advise us as well as be
questioned, held, and seen by us,

what power do you have left to share, if
you become an alone crone?

collected/rising

begin blessing

before i leave the house
i consecrate myself
        dip fingerprint
            into maiden mother crone moon cauldron
            last october's ash
            past coats my fall
a devotee without wreath
            of cedar, pine, willow
greeting today's festival as last day
i submerge into funerals i am destined
grieve with breath i'm not allowed
and permit lungful of sing

deep pussy

we are worlds coming out of worlds
coming out of a world
but there isn't worldwide space within
only a couple inches of arousal
through heavy handing communication
and rapid guttural breathing
rising from plush pockets
where we reposit our ashes
that leak with fired excitement
you don't have to see us
to know we're coming
we're populace's desire
with presence nourishing as streams
flowing ballads from our breast
where we welcome all heads rest
we were born nameless
slid out the lovebox
dressed in cream for this party
prepared at birth
to give birth
before our hips rock oceans on dances floors
before overflow is possible
before letters a, b, and c become more
than finger placements on violin strings
we arrive at sexuality, when they
call it
sell it
oppress it
and we homage unwanted labels
when we use them
if we can say it
we can rename it
as we own no one, but ourselves
and no one owns us
from words to blood flow
everyone wants to swim
within our flow and ebb

where we summer and spring
consoling fallen seeds that burrow
sprouting leaves
regardless of our presentation
heartbeats resonate same
only our scent varies
as home is distinct in voice
as children remembering aroma wail, when separated
as lovers' lush lean speaks endless desire
it is that we're constantly beginning
birthing one another
as womyn turn to each other
deciphering secrets stored
underneath powders and mascara
understanding our first presentation
isn't always a true embrace
but it speaks smoke
and yet we're still learning to speak
speaking to survive
if we're only what we give others
then we should give ourselves everything
a hand held for support
an ear to build voice
a garden to learn our worth
a library to know safety
becoming more than what we've been spoken
as extended, low vibrating, clogged parts
we tuck in, reduce, interrupt, and bleach
instead we believe our needs and receive
making at least one dream
undulating behind eyelids
this reality
so we don't shelve ourselves
and our wisdom feelings
nor foster detached hugs and empty kisses
we women carry as sea
cyclically everyone wants
to swim within

haiti, bless you

a seven days can-
dle lit cyclically, sugar
cane-priestess-rebel

feet

feat

no hurricane thrusts
your drum silent

pools (47)

if we were born to
surrender our resistance,
our fear would cost less

grow/weed along/vine over clenching my own truth

in truth, i intention to be truthful with myself, first. i wear/been gifted/my spirit is housed in an elongated body with 3 ½ cups worth of breasts inherited from my mother, narrow eggplant feet, a polyrhythmic heart—arrhythmia from having consumed prednisone, serevent inhaler causing blackouts, steroid inhaler caused dry mouth (all of which was supposed to prevent/suppress environmentally, stressed related, eating non-african diet induced asthma)—restricted oya lungs, a stomach resisting digestion, when too much wheat-bleached or whole is introduced, two feet of torso, too much legs that do not always cooperated with my eggplants and their baby eggplants so i can walk and not tumble, extraterrestrial limbs, great horn owl eyes, an ass that is not fat enough to see from the front, but is a hill slumping south toward ancestors, smaller melon head—i hate green melon—a squished moorish nose from my dad, non-curly eyebrows my mom drew on me with her eyebrow pencil, after she put it over stove's fire, when she midwifed me from her pussy, under eye bags from being in placenta too long, ears like pagoda lipstick plant's leafs, pussy & head hair feels like wet earth and behaves best when wet—post traumatic enslavement syndrome and past life knowing knows i've drowned too many times to get in water deeper than six feet, womb holds too much memory and cysts herself so she inflames and hasn't been able to resolve her endometriosis, thighs like bread loaves of sprouted grain, knees looking left and right—i haven't discovered who or what they are looking for—palms with short lines—if my dad's mother hadn't died from diet/stress/sadness/environment induced cancer, my mother's mom hadn't died from gangrene caused by pharmaceutical chemicals she ingested for diabetes and kidney failure, which was also induced by pharmaceutical chemicals, and if my great-aunt Ethel Mae hadn't been killed by the white-coats who put an infection breeding, feeding tube in her stomach, after she had a stroke, they would have lived longer than my mom's dad, a ratty tempered bastard whose cousin lived to be 100—my life lines lie, a tummy with a faded diamond shape, hip bones protruding upward keeping watch, when i sleep on my back, and a back peacocking rib ridges. to add braggadocio, i keep a tempest type patience with a wide—mostly drill & bill, silver filled from not brushing my teeth every night—grin, a tongue laying continuously on my mouth's floor because my bones came sowed with silence and by my own will, i harvest my bones' silence similar to earth drinking rain through her pores so subterranean beings slither above her moist—silence slithers another day/turning its day. i effort to shift my twilight, but she/i/my spirit still keeps past life's severed tongue plus my parents' stories from before and union with arrhythmia. am i fascinated with my silences? in truth—i say to myself—i say i am a six-foot body with a half-foot voice, except when intertwining with djundun-sangban-kenkeni. then, i become eighteen feet shouting, cheering, resisting, across floor/wall i was born to grow/weed along/vine over clenching my own truth/truths so i can have other breaths.

where's Betty Mabry Davis

saw you in long beach, california on second street—an insipid, funkless boulevard—inside Fingerprints before 2003, when i was beginning to be a *Nasty Gal*

i was *'vampin trampin'* but incessantly sugarcane hungry. my parents *Shoo-B-Dooped to Motor Booty* with George, Overton and dem so i came from my mom's brickhouse with funk, but

hadn't experienced John Lee Hooker nor your offspring, *Tennessee Slim is the Bomb*. the sugarcane roots were reaching, so i was looking to *Get Picked Up*

amongst riffraff, you sat on the shelf—all self-written, produced and arranged like an avowed funk queen, hair crowning air around your mind, trickily fierce face, a matte-shiny one-piece attire altering your legs toward powder blue platforms that had no performance without you

everybody likes to hang *Bitches* on they wall, when they mention your name, but they fail to allude that *Brew* wouldn't had no tricked-out sauce, if you hadn't put your foot in him

so i paid the cost and took your 1974 home with me. when *Shoo-B-Doop* and *Cop Him* fell upon my spine, i called my midnight train and ask how much would a long stroke, slow ride cost me

Sinaa

our bond, a river upon land
land meeting river
unlocking beckoned low murmurs
spreading as dissipating clouds
with you i believe
in our preservation and legacy
urging a willingness
to vacate scarcity held
ritualistically close
with you, i'm willing to
unlearn shadows' hide
how can i sip liquid faith
affirming this land isn't our land
my body is another's for monopolizing
and our embrace is not ceremonial

how can we subsist

together, we will a breaking
dissipate refuting continuums
as we practice
our embrace, an obsidian self-care
is critical
we are worth this rebellion
and we know our wounds, but
they will not become our nations
because wounded nation(s)
encourage production of replicas
and we are not of a wounded nation
wounded nation(s)
decline to deliberately beautify
the essence of unborn
so unborn may rise beyond
its borderlands, its factures

together we are homeland

lighting candles
with set intentions
and living activated prayers
as we activate the unborn in ourselves
refuse expected refrains
and habitual performances
of traversing ourselves
at expense of drowning within
negating ourselves is easy as living
in a waiting room

i rather be
sentient in our embrace
disturbed by our ancestors
nesting our steady/unsteady accord
in our home on broadway knowing
to our arms
we will always return

dear Sinaa

opening myself to practicing opia is difficult
any variations of willingly showing my wounds stirs my stagnancy

within our moment, when i am asked to not hide myself
makes me long for a latibule where no other being breathes

showing my sutures in progress, self-birthing happening
i am traditionally terrified, it's the one custom solely mine

if not for your valiant high-stepping
                glimmering, darken child-like eyes
                uncut sugarcane energy
                lumbering, loquacious tongue
                operatic caroling
                extroverted negotiating
                listening heart
                scientific and arithmetic estimations
                or deity-fluid and russet flesh

i might have become more house mouse
searching for scraps in the silences

wherever i am, you have a home
wherever there is home, you will always have us

stories great-aunt Ethel keeps

she walks long
with a ledger of past makings
that made her clan
her
me
and other legacies
claiming space as burials
her body
slightly sinks under
at age 86, she covets vibrations
and spits repetitive speak
in protective refrain
she says, *i was so small*
her vocals fluctuate
telling silences she sleeps
her ledger's long
she walks in yesterday's coat
lined with fibers of forest
that was ours, maybe still is
her clan's herstory, ours
holding nests once left
for home elsewhere
of forest singing
our deeds
a paper some of us believe
our generational clan keeps
shadowed by breath
calling me
calling to her
the last of her siblings' clan memory
strolling
after her is us
other legacies
harboring expansions
while renting space
she knows what
i seek

what we seep
she knows
i know she knows
where the deed pushes
back door swinging forth
opening a glimpse
of her brothers
her sister
her father
her mother's early death
her aunt Lydia's mothering
their fertile field
what Lillie sleeps within earth
from which route Glover came to union Lillie
hurt that birthed her first son
trapped narratives
recollections only great-aunt Ethel knows
striped lullabies
that wilted and moved
bringing other children
their children's offspring
us
a continuance of their latches
still latching onto
avoided spaces within our conversations
it's raining down here and *how's everybody*
substitutes for details
in our long distance repetitions
between
mobile, alabama
and
long beach, california
electrical lines of denial
where her vocal symphonies revive
shadows' silenced anger
fear lapsed in birthing
hidden field hollering

crossed arms pulled tight to breasts
theirs
ours
safe keeping
the giggly laughter only she and Lillie wore
great-aunt Ethel knows
what she won't tell beyond
i was so small
is an acceptance i must make
for the voids i'll never know
when she ends our conversations
with *if i find out anything, i'll let you know*
or *i'll call ya*
her ledger becoming ours
parables shaping lineage
where new legacies meet our thruway
made of coded keepings
unknown colors
that time made
that hands made
that we make
continuance of long walks
as her ledger changes
as her ledger changes
us

indigo ~~haiku~~

within ourselves, our
black-indigo selves, is a col-
lection of each other

despite cloudy op-
pression swinging threat, our smi-
les keep us home close

linking us to our-
selves with each other to ourselves
with each other, upon breath

penumbra tableau

returning departure with a penumbra tableau tongue
deities ascending from seabed after midnight
throwing flesh as full moon's oceanic liquid chiffon
speculative fiction in an asthmatically condensed city
fleshed spirits socializing mediums
like patchouli, a potent olfaction abhorred and hungrily lusted
coal black goat skin drumming doundoumba demanding festival truths
ancestral rhythmic possessions and rebellious slang
like strolling cedar trees or newborns' babbling
unbound collections borrowing air as accordion
responding to ineffable stories so adaption drifts
as tobacco smoke wafts stinging eyes
serpent mythology and melanin galaxies
egg shell compacted, however, hatching
in cities cracking, while attempting to chlorinate
the conjures of an unfettered love supreme
closing one world stage opens gates
where another world stages its replica dramas
returning departures reclaim renamed neighborhoods
interjecting words like corridor and plaza
even though the village is known
time and dirty wealth is unable to cleanse
or singe precedents' harping, its strings reach
beyond permitted month to month rentals
where soul vibrates its tree, strolling cedar sings
despite envisioning without the people's heartbeat
elsewhere where quiet segregation
is redistributed, mapped, and textbooked
nor permitting purchase of the land our humanities grew
with yams and the feast of all sacrifices
our celebratory, affectioning bodies
salt water, fire bodies
polyrhythmic, tender, and worshipped bodies
rare books and shea butter bodies
dandy, grand boubou, hoodies and fitted bodies
slick sneaker and manjani bodies
long white tees, and creased jeans bodies

bald fade, mohawk, weaved bodies
tightly coiled hair and bald bodies
pressed, permed, plaited and spiked mane bodies
etcetera and etcetera unnamed, unclaimed bodies
flashing spirit inside a city trying to trash-scrap
people who make it, break it, bend its city body
making it a breathable and employable body
trunks sip origins with cellular memory
where leaves swallow our exhaled
dearly departed bodies
always returning because lifespan has no end
conclusion commences with us

waking up together

to descend upon ourselves

to descend upon yourself
while holding dusk as you dawn
witnessing your brimming rise
necessitates no other approval, but your word

waiting for another's approval
is a brittle aluminum fence overtaken
by a weather of perspective binding
you, a plot, inside someone else's fence
casting you from you, a nation amongst nations

and you, a field of wild nettle, needs water
to liquidate those knowings that aren't your own
for what you know is an ancestral asset
irrigating your rise, bounding past worn posts
attempting to conceal you undetectable
because your dialect is a polyrhythmic reality

where your presence of flesh swept with winds of wisdom
opens a threshold like a smoking bundle
of cedar, pine, and rosemary
so too are the others of us witnessing you
chanting yes
activating your body's water
and transforming any and all dis-ease

in your transformation of believing in you
you begin to starve that uncertainty crackling
every moment another voice douses you with
i don't approve of you as you wish to express
your yawning adoration, your love, but
i'm happy if you're happy
for then you gift back that brittleness
that dry well of thought attempting to bend your being
because you, a vessel clearing the ether with your light
invokes the abundance in the others of us
triggers the wealth with which we stroll

flowers our remembrance that we too
are normal and our gardens shall nourish
and because of you
we too can sever from old ways

spit back those rusted fences
and hold reverence for the medicine that is us

you echo the blessing of rebellion (for Black Lives Matter)
    after Suheir Hammad

you enter the djun-djun-djun beat of street, bending you
snake an atmosphere not ready for the shock of your presence, will

shed history's mark of black, poor, queer, underserved people's want
for appeasement with white house's new color, to

destine your place continuously with each gathering, greet
each high step halting all abuses called normal, you cup the

wind, grasping the last gasp of our slain beloveds' day
you show up, swooping down upon the death elders fear, with

a mirror to our shivers, you echo the blessing of rebellion, a
sermon and chant for unwelcomed cries, chain linking our heart

with every comrades' peacefully clasped arms spurt wisdom, you
an imago believed impossible wills today possible, a will

for freedom we've believed to never shun, a wish
spoken through how many days of continuous protest was

a national call, an olive branch of courage and solidarity, open
dialogues from landlocked state to coast to continents, you

(re)build a movement, an uprising and flag in remembrance will
vibrate, actualize change for generations, want

borderlands removed from our life for our lives rightfully ours, to
believe empowers our spirit, sages our cries, affirms our worth, be

as you are and continue to awaken brave

us kind

us kind
birthed from twilight
we arrive bringing etheric light
from earth's source
divine source of beings like
us kind
embedded with the oldest intonations

when and wherever we enter
us kind stand
us kind perch
us kind resist
us kind rebel
us kind build
us kind glide
whipping atmosphere with our medicines
exchanging chaos for creations freestyle
us kind
activate deep serpents energy
when we
contract breathe
contract breath sweat
contract breath sweat holler
dilation
open

us kind
face and alter the folklore in stories
when our intuition's library is denied
when we're placed in asylums for self-testifying
when our true self is shown as dissipating ripples
we are distilled to a headless pleasure organ
but when we speak, we donate to our revival
embodying holy waters

us kind
learn to surge against dams

exile for safety
earn an alternate economy to altar ourselves, our families
us kind
call upon earth's elements for transformation
organize and activate space for liberation
and when we locate the labyrinth's exit
we contract breathe
contract breath sweat
contract breath sweat holler
dilation
open

us kind
reclaim nations within
as we festival our funerals
and celebrate our complexities
affirming its currency, our currency
our body technology
computes our illustrious wholeness

us kind
live without panhandling existence
for we are calabashes splashing memory
making future memory
we purchase ecstasy with footsteps
gift intentions
sing and holler

us kind
create worlds out of worlds
dance and grieve
birth and labor
commune embracing one another
irrigate our ashes

us kind
transform our realms, when we

contract breathe
contract breath sweat
contract breath sweat holler
dilation
open

falling bodies (two)

black bodies
        black as in
quietest core within earth-womb
where mammon and scientific uncertainties
hasn't a theorized probe
        black as in
when eyes lower at rest
at sorrow
at ecstasy
as in yes, deep spiraling joy
black bodies
        bodies as in
90 percent water towing spirited-flesh
experiences layering as keloids
        as in
bodies following respire falling after thoughts
        as in
tense body with short staccato breathes
        as in
inhale aligning matter between pores and sweat
black bodies read
from a tv-newspaper-online-chatter distance
        these tiny desk perspectives
as falling
        falling as in
failing, losing, dying unnamed martyr
without care for resuscitation
but tiny desk distance perceptions forget
we have these black bodies
our bodies be palindromes
our distance among us
read in front of us
is inner distance within
creates remoteness
with false convictions
not our subscriptions
we chime to our needs

as in no, i don't want this because it feels uncomfortable
as in my right to give or take away your consent to engage with me
as in i can't breathe, when i'm in confined in a chokehold
as in if i die in police custody, i didn't commit suicide
as in prostitution doesn't mean i should be susceptible to rape
as in aborting a baby does not mean i'm a murderer, it means i'm pro- my choice
    and you don't know experiences that have led me here
as in closed mouths willingly not fed on prison hunger strike
as in i'm whole, tender, mesmerizing, complex, infinite love
as i'm not the history, his story, you're fed by which you believe you know me
as in wind affirms me because i have feelings like breeze and hurricane
as in all hands off Assata and bounty removed
as i'm stuck in this structural box, wake the fuck up, stuck in this box, awaken the
    box, and let the box be inferior
as in an orgasm in part of my personal orbit so lick me up consentingly
as in projected phobias signify your inability to rectify borderlands littered with
    your fear
as in slow dance with self—yaaaaaaaaaaaas
as in bombs and war for freedom equals genocide happening now
as in we are all human
black bodies gliding in place
not always falling
yes we do fall
but we never get up alone
we rise together
our breath is eons old
black bodies counted
seen as many falling, that all we do
is fall
    fall
      and fall
        falling to fail
          failing so we fall
in life
in love
in place

in grace
        falling is our place
        is it any person's place to fall
yes fall into our places
        our uses
        our erotic
        our feral hearts' forests
        our inner markets
yes we fall
        into it
        absorbing it
        get into this
        be bound by us
these black bodies alight
what is there to adjust if
        our place is bound
traveling
93 million miles below the sun
900 million miles within moon's pull
being out of place is place
out of place(s)
these black bodies' wounds suture
because there is
        space for all of us
        we hold spaces for each other's spaces
as we pace our complexities
        we deserve healing for ourselves
        ourselves are our communities
we hold pain bladder full
it is our time of release
        it is our time
        it is ours
collect our change
tenderly touch our places
        our center
our center a scion of itself
        birthing us

these black bodies
fluid
crossing over
delving into
unfurling
   beyond our bound bodies
where we is escaping
only pathway is within
   resort into body
   let us fall
beyond exhaustion made from
identifying, explaining, reclaiming, defending
our bodies
to the distant tiny desk
pinholing perspective(s)
that isn't us
instead
      drift into
the constellations sitting
in our black bodies' lap

may the dead in you rise

may the dead in you rise
commune with you
          as though veils to seeing yourself were ground fog, thin and
          vanishing as a hiraeth grief that never was
may you gift yourself
planted squash, pumpkin
and black magic flower seeds
          witnessing yourself, a pit of wholeness
          where you worship yourself, a devotee unto self

Thank You

I acknowledge my Ancestors and their prior journeys living, opening, paving, and brushing the crossroads that allowed *vetiver* to happen: Gladys Giles-Baker, Lillie Mae Osborne-Williams, Ethel Mae Osborne-King and those unnamed.

Because ya'll ensure I respond to my life's call, this book is here. I'm grateful for you mom, Lanette Williams, for being who you are—love and strength filled, tender, resilient, sharp minded, a storyteller and a brilliantly beautiful womyn. You and your sisters, Denise Williams, Deann Williams, Mary Williams, Martha Garner, and Bernice Alexander, relentlessly continue to be a mirror that I look into to become who I am, heal my wounded places, and remember to tell myself yes. Taijhet Nyobi Rockett, Leilani R. Wright, Karla C. Legaspy, Danielle A. Bradford, Shameka L. Cunningham, A.K. Toney, Anastacia-Renee Tolbert, Mike "The Poet" Sonksen, Emma "Art" Kim, Djembe Jan Nicolson, Katrice Jackson, and Meldolphus S. Baker, ya'll are a force in my life. Ching-in Chen, for the inspirations. Vickie Vertiz, for the advice. Lastly, to my wife, Sinaa D. Greene, you put a spell on me with your bravery, passionate speaking, black beauty, compassion, intelligence, your being and endless soapboxing support.

All the communities that have welcomed my in-progresses, my heart prostrates to you. Voices of Our Nations Arts Foundation (VONA/Voices) and Lambda Literary, the ways you gatekeep and allow us to be seen, hold one another and challenge our content is beyond lifesaving. To The Daily Grind, where else would I before midnight? Queen Linda Hollins, for the queer full moon ceremonies and birthing a place for us to connect with earth. AdeRisa Productions, for the spaces you hold, create, and fill-in. Women Who Submit, for the inclusive and encouraging universe you provide. Bayette "Ndella" Davis-Diassy and Dembrebrah West African Drum & Dance Ensemble, for your spirit and presence.

Christen Kincaid and Finishing Line Press, ensuring *vetiver* got its spine. Ya'll rock! Rachel McLeod Kaminer, for digging deeply into my manuscript and editing it. To any person's name I did not recall and list here, please know that I carry you in my body and our spirits hold each other as home. Lastly, thank you Readers and Purchasers, for offering your time and being to exchange, engage, and take in these words. I am humbled you chose this book, made it part of your home, and/or passed it onto another.

May we all continue to rise and grow the medicine within us.

—librecht baker
April 30, 2017

librecht baker is a Long Beach, CA writer. Dembrebrah West African Drum & Dance Ensemble member. English Instructor. VONA/Voices & Lambda Literary Fellow. Sundress Publications' Assistant Editor. MFA in Interdisciplinary Arts from Goddard College. Poetry is included in *Writing the Walls Down: A Convergence of LGBTQ Voices, CHORUS: A Literary Mixtape, Emerge: 2015 Lambda Literary Fellows Anthology, Thank You for Swallowing Volume 2 Issue 2,* and *Solace: Writing Refuge, & LGBTQ Women of Color.* A one-act play, "Lineage Undone," will be part of the 2017 Eastside Queer Stories Festival in Los Angeles.

www.ingramcontent.com/pod-product-compliance
Lightning Source LLC
Chambersburg PA
CBHW070550090426
42735CB00013B/3135